Made in United States
Orlando, FL
09 October 2022

23177837R00055